"Nobody, not even Socrates, has ever asked better questions than Peter Drucker. All the personality, all the wisdom is here to make your work dramatically more effective. There's nothing better. It's like having Peter at your side."

—Bob Buford, author, *Halftime* and *Finishing Well,* and founding chairman, Peter F. Drucker Foundation for Nonprofit Management

"Peter Drucker's penetrating and profound insights are more relevant and needed today than when he originally produced them. This helpful revision of his classic *Self-Assessment Tool* offers managers and leaders in every sector—nonprofit, business, and government—a useful guide to figuring out what's needed, why it matters, and how to make it work. At a time when the need for more effective management and more ethical leadership are the moral equivalent of global warming, Drucker's common sense and courage should be modeled by everyone who cares about doing things right and doing the right thing."

—Ira A. Jackson, dean, Peter F. Drucker and Masatoshi Ito Graduate School of Management, and board member, The Drucker Institute

"Peter Drucker's *Five Most Important Questions* continue to be the indispensable questions that an organization must ask itself, regardless of size or sector, if it is determined to be an organization of the future. When these questions are asked, the journey begins. And as Peter Drucker reminds us in this book, the answers are in the questions."

—Kathy Cloninger, CEO, Girl Scouts of the USA

"The Leader to Leader Institute has done a great service in bringing us this monograph. Good leaders come up with answers, but the great leaders ask the right questions—and this wonderful work helps all leaders do exactly that."
   —Jim Collins, author, *Good to Great and the Social Sectors* and *Built to Last*

"An amazing resource that can help even the most successful organizations become more successful!"
   —Marshall Goldsmith, author, *What Got You Here Won't Get You There: How Successful People Become Even More Successful*, winner of Soundview Executive Summaries' Harold Longman Best Business Book of 2007 Award

The Five

MOST IMPORTANT

Questions

You Will Ever Ask
About Your Organization

Peter F. Drucker
Jim Collins, Philip Kotler, James Kouzes,
Judith Rodin, V. Kasturi Rangan,
and Frances Hesselbein

Leader to Leader
INSTITUTE
Preparing tomorrow's leaders

JOSSEY-BASS
A Wiley Imprint
www.josseybass.com

Published by Jossey-Bass
A Wiley Imprint
989 Market Street, San Francisco, CA 94103-1741—www.josseybass.com

Readers should be aware that Internet Web sites offered as citations and/or sources for further information may have changed or disappeared between the time this was written and when it is read.

Limit of Liability/Disclaimer of Warranty: While the publisher and author have used their best efforts in preparing this book, they make no representations or warranties with respect to the accuracy or completeness of the contents of this book and specifically disclaim any implied warranties of merchantability or fitness for a particular purpose. No warranty may be created or extended by sales representatives or written sales materials. The advice and strategies contained herein may not be suitable for your situation. You should consult with a professional where appropriate. Neither the publisher nor author shall be liable for any loss of profit or any other commercial damages, including but not limited to special, incidental, consequential, or other damages.

Jossey-Bass books and products are available through most bookstores. To contact Jossey-Bass directly call our Customer Care Department within the U.S. at 800-956-7739, outside the U.S. at 317-572-3986, or fax 317-572-4002.

Jossey-Bass also publishes its books in a variety of electronic formats. Some content that appears in print may not be available in electronic books.

Library of Congress Cataloging-in-Publication Data

Drucker, Peter F. (Peter Ferdinand), 1909-2005.
   The five most important questions you will ever ask about your organization/Peter F. Drucker; [with] Jim Collins ... [et al.].
      p. cm. —(Leader to Leader Institute Series)
   "Third edition"—Foreword.
   Includes index.
   ISBN: 978-0-470-22756-5 (pbk.)
   1. Nonprofit organizations—Management—Evaluation. 2. Organizational effectiveness—Evaluation. 3. Total quality management—Evaluation.
   I. Collins, James C. (James Charles). II. Title.
   HD62.6.D777 2008
   658.4'013—dc22   2008009374

Printed in the United States of America
FIRST EDITION
PB Printing   20 19 18 17 16 15 14 13 12

OTHER PUBLICATIONS FROM THE LEADER TO LEADER INSTITUTE

Leader to Leader 2: Enduring Insights on Leadership from the Leader to Leader Institute's Award-Winning Journal, *Frances Hesselbein, Alan Shrader, Editors*

In Extremis Leadership, *Thomas A. Kolditz*

The Leader of the Future 2, *Frances Hesselbein, Marshall Goldsmith, Editors*

Leadership Lessons from West Point, *Major Doug Crandall, Editor*

Leading Organizational Learning: Harnessing the Power of Knowledge, *Marshall Goldsmith, Howard Morgan, Alexander J. Ogg*

Be*Know*Do: Leadership the Army Way, *Frances Hesselbein, General Eric K. Shinseki, Editors*

Hesselbein on Leadership, *Frances Hesselbein*

Peter F. Drucker: An Intellectual Journey (video), *Leader to Leader Institute*

The Collaboration Challenge, *James E. Austin*

Meeting the Collaboration Challenge Workbook, *The Drucker Foundation*

On Leading Change: A Leader to Leader Guide, *Frances Hesselbein Rob Johnston, Editors*

On High Performance Organizations: A Leader to Leader Guide, *Frances Hesselbein, Rob Johnston, Editors*

On Creativity, Innovation, and Renewal: A Leader to Leader Guide, *Frances Hesselbein, Rob Johnston, Editors*

On Mission and Leadership: A Leader to Leader Guide, *Frances Hesselbein, Rob Johnston, Editors*

Leading for Innovation, *Frances Hesselbein, Marshall Goldsmith, Iain Somerville, Editors*

Leading in a Time of Change (video), *Peter F. Drucker, Peter M. Senge, Frances Hesselbein*

Leading in a Time of Change Viewer's Workbook, *Peter F. Drucker, Peter M. Senge, Frances Hesselbein*

Leading Beyond the Walls, *Frances Hesselbein, Marshall Goldsmith, Iain Somerville, Editors*

The Organization of the Future, *Frances Hesselbein, Marshall Goldsmith, Richard Beckhard, Editors*

The Community of the Future, *Frances Hesselbein, Marshall Goldsmith, Richard Beckhard, Richard F. Schubert, Editors*

Leader to Leader: Enduring Insights on Leadership from the Drucker Foundation, *Frances Hesselbein, Paul Cohen, Editors*

The Drucker Foundation Self-Assessment Tool: Participant Workbook, *Peter F. Drucker*

The Drucker Foundation Self-Assessment Tool Process Guide, *Gary J. Stern*

Excellence in Nonprofit Leadership (video), *Featuring Peter F. Drucker, Max De Pree, Frances Hesselbein, Michele Hunt; Moderated by Richard F. Schubert*

Excellence in Nonprofit Leadership Workbook *and* Facilitator's Guide, *Peter F. Drucker Foundation for Nonprofit Management*

Lessons in Leadership (video), *Peter F. Drucker*

Lessons in Leadership Workbook *and* Facilitator's Guide, *Peter F. Drucker*

The Leader of the Future, *Frances Hesselbein, Marshall Goldsmith, Richard Beckhard, Editors*

Find additional resources, helpful tools, and
information on *The Five Most Important Questions* at
www.fivequestionsbook.com

CONTENTS

Transformational Leadership   77
Frances Hesselbein

The Self-Assessment Process   83

Suggested Questions to Explore   87

FOREWORD

It is often said that the simple questions are the hardest to answer. But how could this be? Doesn't logic tell us that simple questions should also be the easiest to answer? No. Simple questions can be profound, and answering them requires us to make stark and honest—and sometimes painful—self-assessments. We do a great disservice to our organizations—whether business, nonprofit, or public sector—and to our customers and to ourselves if we do not ask these five simple yet profound essential questions first posed by Peter F. Drucker.

As Peter Drucker said in the first edition of *The Five Most Important Questions You Will Ever Ask About Your Nonprofit Organization,* "The most important aspect of the Self-Assessment Tool is the questions it poses. Answers are important; you need answers because you need action. But the most important thing is to ask these questions."[1]

More than fifteen years ago, the Leader to Leader Institute set off on a journey. Then known as the Peter F. Drucker Foundation for Nonprofit Management, the mission was *to help the social sector achieve excellence in performance and build responsible citizenship.* The immediate and compelling question we heard from our customers when we began our work was, "You say we should achieve excellence, but how do we know when we get there?" That began our journey, together with our customer-partners, to develop a strategic organizational self-assessment tool.

Much excellent work was done by exuberant volunteers, staff, facilitators, and organizations—collaborating, developing, testing, publishing, and distributing the first edition of *The Five Most Important Questions.* Yet at its core was the management philosophy of Peter F. Drucker. If Peter Drucker were with you and your organization today, we believe he would ask the same questions of you that he asked more than fifteen years ago:

1. What is our mission?
2. Who is our customer?
3. What does the customer value?
4. What are our results?
5. What is our plan?[2]

These five simple—yet complex and compelling—questions are as essential and relevant today as they were then. These questions used as a self-assessment tool are unique, and though first developed in this framework for social sector organizations, they can be applied to almost any organization today. This book is designed to be used for *organizational* strategic self-assessment, not for *program* assessment or for an *individual* performance review. It starts with the fundamental question *What is our mission?* It addresses the question of the organization's reason for being—its purpose—not the *how*. The mission inspires; it is what you want your organization to be remembered for. The questions then guide you through the process of assessing *how well you are doing,* ending with a measurable, results-focused strategic plan to further the mission and to achieve the organization's goals, guided by the vision.

The ultimate beneficiaries of this very simple process are the people or customers touched by your organization and by others like you who have made the courageous decision to look within yourselves and your organization, identify strengths and challenges, embrace change, foster innovation, accept and respond to customer feedback, look beyond the organization for trends and opportunities, encourage planned abandonment, and demand measurable results. Some organizations of the past rested on good deeds alone. Organizations of the future are relevant and sustainable with measurable results.

This self-assessment model is flexible and adaptable. Walk this tool into any boardroom or CEO's office. Use it in any sector—public, private, or social. It does not matter whether the organization is a Fortune 500 multinational or a small entrepreneurial start-up; a large national government agency or one that serves your local town or regional heartland; a billion-dollar nonprofit foundation or a $100,000 homeless shelter. What matters is commitment to the future, commitment to the customer, commitment to the mission, and commitment to the process. Self-discovery is an introspective and coura-geous journey that gives organizations and leaders the en-ergy and courage to grow.

Fifteen years ago, *The Five Most Important Questions* was powerful, relevant—the indispensable tool for organizations determined to be viable, the organization of the future. Peter Drucker and the then Drucker Foundation launched a self-assessment tool exactly right for the moment, written within the context of the times—the early 1990s.

Today, in the new edition of the indispensable tool, once again we have considered the context of our times. As we are approaching a new decade—different context, different backdrop—*The Five Most Important Questions,* once again, is essential, relevant, and responsive to the needs of leaders and organizations in our own times. And, once again, the father of modern management leads the way into the future.

We could not be more grateful for the generous contri-butions of five of the most respected and admired thought leaders of our time:

- Jim Collins, who describes how an organization's mission reflects the fundamental tension between continuity and change, and how organizations particularly good at adapting to change know what should *not* change
- Philip Kotler, who implores us to do a better job of understanding who our target customers are, and then

to deeply please them instead of trying to casually
please everyone
- Jim Kouzes, who suggests that everything exemplary
leaders do is about creating value for their customers
- Judith Rodin, who asserts that no plan can be
considered complete—or satisfactory—until it produces
measurable outcomes and incorporates mechanisms
that allow midcourse corrections based on results
- V. Kasturi Rangan, who describes what makes a good
plan and the importance of monitoring plan execution
and closing the feedback loop for the next planning cycle

You will be inspired and enlightened by their thoughtful
contributions, and we know you will be as appreciative of
their generous gifts of wisdom, experience, and intellectual
energy as we are. The original *The Five Most Important Questions* emerged from the wisdom of Peter Drucker. We once
again share Peter's wisdom with you, and enrich the tool
with the thoughts of these five great leaders. We are deeply
grateful to you, our readers and supporters, fellow travelers
on the journey to organizational self-discovery.

❖

Frances Hesselbein
Chairman and founding president
President and CEO
Leader to Leader Institute
New York City

NOTES

1. Peter F. Drucker, *The Five Most Important Questions You Will Ever Ask About Your Nonprofit Organization* (San Francisco: Jossey-Bass, 1993), p. 3.
2. Drucker, *The Five Most Important Questions,* p. viii.

ABOUT PETER F. DRUCKER

Peter F. Drucker (1909–2005)—widely considered to be the world's foremost pioneer of management theory—was a writer, teacher, and consultant specializing in strategy and policy for businesses and social sector organizations. Drucker's career as a writer, consultant, and teacher spanned nearly seventy-five years. His groundbreaking work turned modern management theory into a serious discipline. He has influenced or created nearly every facet of its application, including decentralization, privatization, empowerment, and understanding of "the knowledge worker." He is the author of thirty-one books, which have been translated into more than twenty languages. Thirteen books deal with society, economics, and politics; fifteen deal with management. Two of his books are novels, one is autobiographical, and he is coauthor of a book on Japanese painting. He has made four series of educational films based on his management books. He has been an editorial columnist for the *Wall Street Journal* and a frequent contributor to the *Harvard Business Review* and other periodicals.

Drucker was born in 1909 in Vienna and was educated there and in England. He took his doctorate in public and international law while working as a newspaper reporter in Frankfurt, Germany. He then worked as an economist for an international bank in London. Drucker moved to London in 1933 to escape Hitler's Germany and took a job as a securities analyst for an insurance firm. Four years later, he married Doris Schmitz, and the couple departed for the United States in 1937.

Drucker landed a part-time teaching position at Sarah Lawrence College in New York in 1939. He joined the faculty of Bennington College in Vermont as professor of politics and philosophy in 1942, and the next year put his academic career on hold to spend two years studying the management structure of General Motors. This experience led to his book *Concept of the Corporation,* an immediate best-seller in the United States and Japan, which validated the notion that great companies could stand among humankind's noblest inventions. For more than twenty years, he was professor of management at the Graduate Business School of New York University. He was awarded the Presidential Citation, the university's highest honor.

Drucker came to California in 1971, where he was instrumental in the development of the country's first executive MBA program for working professionals at Claremont Graduate University (then known as Claremont Graduate

School). The university's management school was named the Peter F. Drucker Graduate School of Management in his honor in 1987. He taught his last class at the school in the spring of 2002. His courses consistently attracted the largest number of students of any class offered by the university.

As a consultant, Drucker specialized in strategy and policy for governments, businesses, and nonprofit organizations. His special focus was on the organization and work of top management. He worked with some of the world's largest businesses and with small and entrepreneurial companies. In recent years, he worked extensively with nonprofit organizations, including universities, hospitals, and churches. He served as a consultant to a number of agencies of the U.S. government and with the governments of Canada, Japan, Mexico, and other nations throughout the world.

Peter Drucker has been hailed in the United States and abroad as the seminal thinker, writer, and lecturer on the contemporary organization. Drucker's work has had a major influence on modern organizations and their management over the past sixty years. Valued for keen insight and the ability to convey his ideas in popular language, Drucker has often set the agenda in management thinking. Central to his philosophy is the view that people are an organization's most valuable resource and that a manager's job is to prepare and free people to perform. In 1997, he was featured on the cover of *Forbes* magazine under the headline "Still the Youngest Mind," and *BusinessWeek* has called him "the most enduring management thinker of our time."

On June 21, 2002, Peter Drucker, author of *The Effective Executive* and *Management Challenges for the 21st Century,* received the Presidential Medal of Freedom from President George W. Bush.

Drucker received honorary doctorates from numerous universities around the world, including the United States, Belgium, Czechoslovakia, Great Britain, Japan, Spain, and Switzerland. He was honorary chairman of the Leader to Leader Institute. He passed away on November 11, 2005, at age ninety-five.

WHY SELF-ASSESSMENT?

Peter F. Drucker

The ninety million volunteers who work for nonprofit institutions—America's largest employer—exemplify the American commitment to responsible citizenship in the community. Indeed, nonprofit organizations are central to the quality of life in America and are its most distinguishing feature.[1]

Forty years ago management was a very bad word in nonprofit organizations. Management meant *business,* and the one thing a nonprofit was not was a *business.* Today, nonprofits understand that they need management all the more because they have no conventional bottom line. Now they need to learn how to use management so they can concentrate on their mission. Yet, there are few tools available that address the distinct characteristics and central needs of the many nonprofit organizations in America.[2]

Although I don't know a single for-profit business that is as well managed as a few of the nonprofits, the great majority of the nonprofits can be graded a "C" at best. Not for lack of effort; most of them work very hard. But for lack of *focus,* and for lack of *tool competence.* I predict that this will change, however, and we at the Drucker Foundation [now Leader to Leader Institute] hope to make our greatest impact in these areas of focus and tool competence.[3]

For years, most nonprofits felt that good intentions were by themselves enough. But today, we know that because we don't have a bottom line, we have to manage *better* than for-profit business. We have to have discipline rooted in our mission. We have to manage our limited resources of people and money for maximum effectiveness. And we have to think through very clearly what results are for our organization.[4]

THE FIVE MOST IMPORTANT QUESTIONS

The self-assessment process is a method for assessing what you are doing, why you are doing it, and what you *must* do to improve an organization's performance. It asks the five essential questions: *What is our mission? Who is our customer? What does the customer value? What are our results?* and *What is our plan?* Self-assessment leads to action and lacks meaning without it. To meet growing needs and succeed in a turbulent and exacting environment, social sector organizations must focus on mission, demonstrate accountability, and achieve results.[5]

The self-assessment tool forces an organization to focus on its mission. About eight out of ten nonprofits in the country are small organizations whose leaders find it very hard to say no when someone comes to them with a good cause. I advised some close friends of mine, working with a local council of churches, that half the things they are doing they shouldn't be doing—not because they're unimportant but because they're not needed. I told them, "Other people can do those activities and do them well. Maybe a few years ago it was a good idea for you to help get this farmers' market started because those Vietnamese farmers in your area needed a place to sell their produce; but it's going well now, and you don't have to run it anymore. It's time for organized abandonment."[6]

You cannot arrive at the right definition of results without significant input from your *customers*—and please do not get into a debate over that term. In business, a customer is someone you must satisfy. If you don't, you have no results. And pretty soon you have no business. In a nonprofit organization, whether you call the customer a student, patient, member, participant, volunteer, donor, or anything else, the focus must be on what these individuals and groups value—on satisfying their needs, wants, and aspirations.[7]

The danger is in acting on what *you* believe satisfies the customer. You will inevitably make wrong assumptions. Leadership should not even try to guess at the answers; it should always go to customers in a systematic quest for those answers. And so, in the self-assessment process, you will have a three-way conversation with your board, staff, and customers and include each of these perspectives in your discussions and decisions.[8]

PLANNING IS NOT AN EVENT

When you follow the self-assessment process through to its completion, you will have formulated a plan. Planning is frequently misunderstood as making future decisions, but decisions exist only in the present. You must have overarching goals that add up to a vision for the future, but the immediate question that faces the organization is not what to do tomorrow. The question is, What must we do *today* to achieve results? Planning is not an event. It is the continuous process of strengthening what works and abandoning what does not, of making risk-taking decisions with the greatest knowledge of their potential effect, of setting objectives, appraising performance and results through systematic feedback, and making ongoing adjustments as conditions change.[9]

ENCOURAGE CONSTRUCTIVE DISSENT

All the first-rate decision makers I've observed had a very simple rule: If you have quick consensus on an important matter, don't make the decision. Acclamation means nobody has done the homework. The organization's decisions are important and risky, and they *should* be controversial. There is a very old saying—it goes all the way to Aristotle and later became an axiom of the early Christian Church: In essentials unity, in action freedom, and in all things trust. Trust requires that dissent come out in the open.[10]

Nonprofit institutions need a healthy atmosphere for dissent if they wish to foster innovation and commitment. Nonprofits must encourage honest and constructive disagreement precisely because everybody is committed to a good cause: Your opinion versus mine can easily be taken as your good faith versus mine. Without proper encouragement, people have a tendency to avoid such difficult, but vital, discussions or turn them into underground feuds.[11]

Another reason to encourage dissent is that any organization needs its nonconformist. This is not the kind of person who says, "There is a right way and a wrong way—and our way." Rather, he or she asks, "What is the right way *for the future?*" and is ready to change. Finally, open discussion uncovers what the objections are. With genuine participation, a decision doesn't need to be sold. Suggestions can be incorporated, objections addressed, and the decision itself becomes a commitment to action.[12]

CREATING TOMORROW'S SOCIETY OF CITIZENS

Your commitment to self-assessment is a commitment to developing yourself and your organization as a leader. You will expand your vision by listening to your customers, by encouraging constructive dissent, by looking at the sweeping transformation taking place in society. You have vital judgments ahead: whether to change the mission, whether to abandon programs that have outlived their usefulness and concentrate resources elsewhere, how to match opportunities with your competence and commitment, *how you will build community and change lives*. Self-assessment is the first action requirement of leadership: the constant resharpening, constant refocusing, never being really satisfied. And the time to do this is when you are successful. If you wait until things start to go down, then it's very difficult.[13]

We are creating tomorrow's society of citizens through the social sector, through *your* nonprofit organization. And in that society, everybody is a leader, everybody is responsible, everybody acts. Therefore, mission and leadership are not just things to read about, to listen to; they are things to *do* something about. Self-assessment can and should convert good intentions and knowledge into effective action—not next year but tomorrow morning.[14]

Notes

1. Peter F. Drucker, *The Five Most Important Questions You Will Ever Ask About Your Nonprofit Organization* (San Francisco: Jossey-Bass, 1993), SAT1: p. 2.

2. Drucker, *The Five Most Important Questions,* p. 2.

3. Drucker, *The Five Most Important Questions,* p. 2.

4. Drucker, *The Five Most Important Questions,* p. 2.

5. Gary J. Stern, *The Drucker Foundation Self-Assessment Tool: Process Guide* (San Francisco: Jossey-Bass, 1999), SAT2PG: p. 4.

6. Drucker, *The Five Most Important Questions,* p. 3.

7. Stern, *The Drucker Foundation Self-Assessment Tool: Process Guide,* p. 4.

8. Stern, *The Drucker Foundation Self-Assessment Tool: Process Guide,* p. 4.

9. Stern, *The Drucker Foundation Self-Assessment Tool: Process Guide,* p. 4.

10. Peter F. Drucker, *The Drucker Foundation Self-Assessment Tool: Participant Workbook* (San Francisco: Jossey-Bass, 1999), SAT2: p. 5.
11. Drucker, *The Drucker Foundation Self-Assessment Tool: Participant Workbook*, p. 6.
12. Drucker, *The Drucker Foundation Self-Assessment Tool: Participant Workbook*, p. 6.
13. Drucker, *The Drucker Foundation Self-Assessment Tool: Participant Workbook*, p. 6.
14. Drucker, *The Drucker Foundation Self-Assessment Tool: Participant Workbook*, p. 6.

❖

What Is Our Mission?

Question 1

WHAT IS OUR MISSION?

Peter F. Drucker

* What is the current mission?

* What are our challenges?

* What are our opportunities?

* Does the mission need to be revisited?

ach social sector institution exists to make a distinctive difference in the lives of individuals and in society. Making this difference is the mission—the organization's purpose and very reason for being. Each of more than one million nonprofit organizations in the United States may have a very different mission, but *changing lives* is always the starting point and ending point. A mission cannot be impersonal; it has to have deep meaning, be something you believe in—something you know is right. A fundamental responsibility of leadership is to make sure that everybody knows the mission, understands it, lives it.

Many years ago, I sat down with the administrators of a major hospital to think through the mission of the emergency room. As do most hospital administrators, they began by saying, "Our mission is health care." And that's the wrong definition. The hospital does not take care of health; the hospital takes care of illness. It took us a long time to come up with the very simple and (most people thought) too-obvious statement that the emergency room was there *to give assurance to the afflicted.* To do that well, you had to know what really went on. And, to the surprise of the physicians and nurses, the function of a good emergency room in their community was to tell eight out of ten people there was nothing wrong that a good night's sleep wouldn't fix. "You've been shaken up. Or the baby has the flu. All right, it's got convulsions, but there is nothing seriously wrong with the child." The doctors and nurses gave assurance.

We worked it out, but it sounded awfully obvious. Yet translating the mission into action meant that everybody who came in was seen by a qualified person in less than a minute. The first objective was to see everybody, almost immediately—because that is the only way to give assurance.

IT SHOULD FIT ON A T-SHIRT

The effective mission statement is short and sharply focused. It should fit on a T-shirt. The mission says *why* you do what you do, not the means by which you do it. The mission is broad, even eternal, yet directs you to do the right things now and into the future so that everyone in the organization can say, "What I am doing contributes to the goal." So it must be clear, and it must inspire. Every board member, volunteer, and staff person should be able to see the mission and say, "Yes. This is something I want to be remembered for."

To have an effective mission, you have to work out an exacting match of your opportunities, competence, and commitment. Every good mission statement reflects all three. You look first at the outside environment. The organization that starts from the inside and then tries to find places to put its resources is going to fritter itself away. Above all, it will focus on yesterday. Demographics change. Needs change. You must search out the accomplished facts—things that have already happened—that present challenges and opportunities for the organization. Leadership has no choice but to anticipate the future and attempt to mold it, bearing in mind that whoever is content to rise with the tide will also fall with it. It is not given to mortals to do any of these things well, but, lacking divine guidance, you must still assess where your opportunity lies.

Look at the state of the art, at changing conditions, at competition, the funding environment, at gaps to be filled. The hospital isn't going to sell shoes, and it's not going into education on a big scale. It's going to take care of the sick. But the specific aim may change. Things that are of primary importance now may become secondary or totally irrelevant very soon. With the limited resources you have—and I don't just mean people and money but also competence—where can you dig in and make a difference? Where can you set a new standard of performance? What really inspires your commitment?

MAKE PRINCIPLED DECISIONS

One cautionary note: *Never subordinate the mission in order to get money.* If there are opportunities that threaten the integrity of the organization, you must say no. Otherwise, you sell your soul. I sat in on a discussion at a museum that had been offered a donation of important art on conditions that no self-respecting museum could possibly accept. Yet a few board members said, "Let's take the donation. We can change the conditions down the road." "No, that's unconscionable!" others responded, and the board fought over the issue. They finally agreed they would lose too much by compromising basic principles to please a donor. The board forfeited some very nice pieces of sculpture, but core values had to come first.

KEEP THINKING IT THROUGH

Keep the central question What is our mission? in front of you throughout the self-assessment process. Step by step you will analyze challenges and opportunities, identify your customers, learn what they value, and define your results. When it is time to develop the plan, you will take all that you have learned and revisit the mission to affirm or change it.

As you begin, consider this wonderful sentence from a sermon of that great poet and religious philosopher of the seventeenth century, John Donne: "Never start with tomorrow to reach eternity. Eternity is not being reached by small steps." We start with the long range and then feed back and say, "What do we do *today?*" The ultimate test is not the beauty of the mission statement. The ultimate test is your performance.

Note

The preceding text is from Peter F. Drucker, *The Drucker Foundation Self-Assessment Tool: Participant Workbook* (San Francisco: Jossey-Bass, 1999), SAT2, pp. 14–16.

Question 1

WHAT IS OUR MISSION?

Jim Collins

What is our mission? Such a simple question—but it goes right to the heart of the fundamental tension in any great institution: the dynamic interplay between continuity and change. Every truly great organization demonstrates the characteristic of *preserve the core, yet stimulate progress.* On the one hand, it is guided by a set of core values and fundamental purpose—a core mission that changes little or not at all over time; and, on the other hand, it stimulates progress: change, improvement, innovation, renewal. The core mission remains fixed while operating practices, cultural norms, strategies, tactics, processes, structures, and methods continually change in response to changing realities. Indeed, the great paradox of change is that the organizations that best adapt to a changing world first and foremost know what should *not* change; they have a fixed anchor of guiding principles around which they can more easily change everything else.

They know the difference between what is truly sacred and what is not, between what should never change and what should be always open for change, between "what we stand for" and "how we do things."

The best universities understand, for example, that the ideal of freedom of inquiry must remain intact as a guiding precept while the operating practice of tenure goes through inevitable change and revision. The most enduring churches understand that the core ideology of the religion must remain fixed while the specific practices and venues of worship change in response to the realities of younger generations. Mission as Drucker thought of it provides the glue that holds an organization together as it expands, decentralizes, globalizes, and attains diversity. Think of it as analogous to the principles of Judaism that held the Jewish people together for centuries without a homeland, even as they scattered throughout the Diaspora. Or think of the truths held to be self-evident in the U.S. Declaration of Independence, or the enduring ideals of the scientific community that bond scientists from every nationality together with the common aim of advancing knowledge.

Your core mission provides guidance, not just about what to do, but equally what *not* to do. Social sector leaders pride themselves on "doing good" for the world, but to be of maximum service requires a ferocious focus on doing good *only* if it fits your mission. To do the most good requires saying no to pressures to stray, and the discipline to stop doing what does not fit. When Frances Hesselbein led the Girl

Scouts of the USA, she pounded out a simple mantra: "We are here for only one reason: to help a girl reach her highest potential." She steadfastly steered the Girl Scouts into those activities—and only those activities—where it could make a unique and significant contribution of value to its members. When a charity organization sought to partner with the Girl Scouts, envisioning an army of smiling girls going door to door to canvass for the greater good, Hesselbein commended the desire to make a difference, but gave a polite and firm no. Just because something is a "once-in-a-lifetime opportunity"—even a once-in-a-lifetime funding opportunity—is merely a fact, not necessarily a reason to act. If a great opportunity does not fit your mission, then the answer must be "Thank you, but no."

The question of mission has become, if anything, even more important as our world becomes increasingly disruptive and turbulent. No matter how much the world changes, people still have a fundamental need to belong to something they can feel proud of. They have a fundamental need for guiding values and sense of purpose that give their life and work meaning. They have a fundamental need for connection to other people, sharing with them the common bond of beliefs and aspirations. They have a desperate need for a guiding philosophy, a beacon on the hill to keep in sight during dark and disruptive times. More than any time in the past, people will demand operating autonomy—freedom plus responsibility—and will simultaneously demand that the organizations of which they are a part *stand* for something.

❖

Who Is Our Customer?

Question 2

WHO IS OUR CUSTOMER?

Peter F. Drucker

- ❖ Who is our primary customer?
- ❖ Who are our supporting customers?
- ❖ How will our customers change?

ot long ago, the word *customer* was rarely heard in the social sector. Nonprofit leaders would say, "We don't have customers. That's a marketing term. We have clients . . . recipients . . . patients. We have audience members. We have students." Rather than debate language, I ask, "Who must be satisfied for the organization to achieve results?" When you answer this question, you define your customer as one who values your service, who wants what you offer, who feels it's important to *them*.

Social sector organizations have two types of customers. The *primary* customer is the person whose life is changed through your work. Effectiveness requires focus, and that means *one* response to the question, Who is our primary customer? Those who chase off in too many directions suffer by diffusing their energies and diminishing their performance. *Supporting customers* are volunteers, members, partners, funders, referral sources, employees, and others who must be satisfied. They are all people who can say no, people who have the choice to accept or reject what you offer. You might satisfy them by providing the opportunity for meaningful service, by directing contributions toward results you both believe in, by joining forces to meet community needs.

The primary customer is never the *only* customer, and to satisfy one customer without satisfying the others means there is no performance. This makes it very tempting to say there is more than one primary customer, but effective organizations resist this temptation and keep to a focus—the primary customer.

IDENTIFY THE PRIMARY CUSTOMER

Let me give you a positive example of identifying and concentrating on the primary customer in a complex setting. A mid-sized nonprofit organization's mission is *to increase people's economic and social independence.* They have twenty-five programs considered to be in four different fields, but for thirty-five years they have focused on only one primary customer: *the person with multiple barriers to employment.* In the beginning, this meant the physically handicapped. Today, it still means people with disabilities but also single mothers who want to be finished with welfare, older workers who have been laid off, people with chronic and persistent mental illness living in the community, and those struggling against long-term chemical dependency. Each belongs to a single primary customer group: the person with multiple barriers to employment. Results are measured in every program by whether the customer can now gain and keep productive work.

The primary customer is not necessarily someone you can reach, someone you can sit down with and talk to directly. Primary customers may be infants, or endangered species, or members of a future generation. Whether or not you can have an active dialogue, identifying the primary customer puts your priorities in order and gives you a reference point for critical decisions on the organization's values.

IDENTIFYING SUPPORTING CUSTOMERS

The Girl Scouts of United States of America is the largest girls' and women's organization in the world and a nonprofit that exemplifies service to one primary customer—the girl—balanced with satisfaction of many supporting customers, all of whom change over time. A long-held Girl Scouts priority is offering equal access to every girl in the United States. This has not changed since 1912 when the Girl Scouts founder said, "I have something for all the girls." Frances Hesselbein, at the time she was national executive director (1976–1990), told me, "We look at the projections and understand that by the year 2000, one-third of this country will be members of minority groups. Many people are very apprehensive about the future and what this new racial and ethnic composition will mean. We see it as an unprecedented opportunity to reach all girls with a program that will help them in their growing-up years, which are more difficult than ever before."

Reaching a changing primary customer means a new view of supporting customers. Frances explained, "In a housing project with no Girl Scout troop there are hundreds of young girls really needing this kind of program, and families wanting something better for their children. It is important as we reach out to girls in every racial and economic group to understand the very special needs, the culture, the readiness of each group. We work with many supporting customers; with the clergy perhaps, with the director of that housing project, with parents—a group of people from that particular community. We recruit leaders, train them right there. We have to demonstrate our respect for that community, our interest in it. Parents have to know it will be a positive experience for their daughters."

KNOW YOUR CUSTOMERS

Customers are never static. There will be greater or lesser numbers in the groups you already serve. They will become more diverse. Their needs, wants, and aspirations will evolve. There may be entirely new customers you must satisfy to achieve results—individuals who really need the service, want the service, but not in the way in which it is available today. And there are customers you should *stop* serving because the organization has filled a need, because people can be better served elsewhere, or because you are not producing results.

Answering the question Who is our customer? provides the basis for determining what customers value, defining your results, and developing the plan. Yet, even after careful thought, customers may surprise you; then you must be prepared to adjust. I remember one of my pastoral friends saying of a new program, "Great, a wonderful program for the newly married." The program was indeed a success. But to the consternation of the young assistant pastor who designed it and ran it, not a single newly married couple enrolled. All the participants were young people living together and wondering whether they should get married. And the senior pastor had a terrible time with his brilliant young assistant, who became righteous and said, "We haven't designed it for them!" He wanted to throw them out.

Often, the customer is one step ahead of you. So you must *know your customer*—or quickly get to know them. Time and again you will have to ask, "Who is our customer?" because customers constantly change. The organization that is devoted to results—always with regard to its basic integrity—will adapt and change as they do.

Note

The preceding text is from Peter F. Drucker, *The Drucker Foundation Self-Assessment Tool: Participant Workbook* (San Francisco: Jossey-Bass, 1999), SAT2, pp. 22–24.

Question 2

WHO IS OUR CUSTOMER?

Philip Kotler

Peter Drucker told us over forty years ago, "The purpose of a company is to create a customer. . . . The only profit center is the customer." Jack Welch, former CEO of General Electric, drove the same point home to his employees: "Nobody can guarantee your job. Only customers can guarantee your job."

In the Internet age, when customers have so much more information and are daily exchanging opinions with each other, companies are finally waking up to the idea that they have a new boss: the customer. A perceptive Ford executive at one time said, "If we're not customer driven, our cars won't be either." Apparently the Ford company didn't listen to this executive.

If Peter Drucker were here today, he would amend his observation. He would say, "The best companies don't create customers. They create fans." He would say that it is less important to report better profits this year than to check on whether you improved your share of the customer's mind and heart this year.

We must do a better job of understanding who the customer is. The old thinking was that customers would hear about us and, we hope, choose our products. The new thinking is that we, the company, choose our customers. We even may refuse to do business with certain customers. Our business is not to casually please everyone, but to deeply please our target customers.

So the first job is to define our target customers. This definition will affect everything: the designing of our product and its features, the choice of our distribution outlets, the crafting of our messages, the choice of our media, and the setting of our prices.

In order to define our customer, we must take a broader view of the buying process. The purchase of anything is the result of several roles being played. Consider the purchase of a new family automobile. The *initiator* might have been a family friend who mentioned an impressive new car. The teenage son might have been an *influencer* of the type of car to consider. The *decider* might be the wife. The *buyer* might be the husband.

The marketer's job is to identify these roles and use the limited marketing resources to reach the most influential people involved in the final decision. Marketers and salespeople need skills in mapping the perceptions, preferences, and values of the different players in the decision-making process.

Many companies have adopted *customer relationship management,* meaning that they collect loads of information about transactions and encounters with their customers. Most pharmaceutical firms, for example, have deep information on individual physicians and their values and preferences. Increasingly, however, we are recognizing that this information is not enough. It doesn't capture the quality of the *customer experience.* Simply managing data about customers is no substitute for ensuring that the customers are satisfied with their experience of the company. An old Chinese proverb says, "If you cannot smile, do not open a shop."

So in the end, we must master our knowledge of who are the target customers, who and what influences them, and how to create highly satisfying customer experiences. Recognize that today's customers are increasingly buying on value, not on relationship. Your success ultimately depends on what you have contributed to the success of your customers.

❖

What Does the Customer Value?

Question 3

WHAT DOES THE CUSTOMER VALUE?

Peter F. Drucker

❖ What do we believe our primary and
   supporting customers value?
❖ What knowledge do we need to gain
   from our customers?
❖ How will I participate in gaining this
   knowledge?

he question, What do customers value?—what satisfies their needs, wants, and aspirations—is so complicated that it can only be answered by customers themselves. And the first rule is that there are no irrational customers. Almost without exception, customers behave rationally in terms of their own realities and their own situation. Leadership should not even try to guess at the answers but should always go to the customers in a systematic quest for those answers. I practice this. Each year I personally telephone a random sample of fifty or sixty students who graduated ten years earlier. I ask, "Looking back, what did we contribute in this school? What is still important to you? What should we do better? What should we stop doing?" And believe me, the knowledge I have gained has had a profound influence.

What does the customer value? may be the most important question. Yet it is the one least often asked. Nonprofit leaders tend to answer it for themselves. "It's the quality of our programs. It's the way we improve the community." People are so convinced they are doing the right things and so committed to their cause that they come to see the institution as an end in itself. But that's a bureaucracy. Instead of asking, "Does it deliver value to our customers?" they ask,

"Does it fit our rules?" And that not only inhibits performance but also destroys vision and dedication.

UNDERSTAND YOUR ASSUMPTIONS

My friend Philip Kotler, a professor at Northwestern University, points out that many organizations are very clear about the value they would like to deliver, but they often don't understand that value from the perspective of their customers. They make assumptions based on their own interpretation. So begin with assumptions and find out what *you* believe your customers value. Then you can compare these beliefs with what customers actually are saying, find the differences, and go on to assess your results.

WHAT DOES THE PRIMARY CUSTOMER VALUE?

Learning what their primary customers value led to significant change in a homeless shelter. The shelter's existing beliefs about value added up to nutritious meals and clean beds. A series of face-to-face interviews with their homeless customers was arranged, and both board and staff members took part. They found out that yes, the food and beds are appreciated but do little or nothing to satisfy the deep aspiration *not to be homeless*. The customers said, "We need a place of safety from which to rebuild our lives, a place we can at least temporarily call a real home." The organization threw out their assumptions and their old rules. They said, "How can we make this shelter a safe haven?" They eliminated the fear that comes with being turned back on the street each morning. They now make it possible to stay at the shelter quite a while, and work with individuals to find out what a rebuilt life means to them and how they can be helped to realize their goal.

The new arrangement also requires more of the customer. Before, it was enough to show up hungry. Now, to get what the customer values most, he must make a commitment. He must work on his problems and plans in order to stay on. The customer's stake in the relationship is greater, as are the organization's results.

WHAT DO SUPPORTING CUSTOMERS VALUE?

Your knowledge of what primary customers value is of utmost importance. Yet the reality is, unless you understand equally what supporting customers value, you will not be able to put all the necessary pieces in place for the organization to perform. In social sector organizations there have always been a multitude of supporting customers, in some cases each with a veto power. A school principal has to satisfy teachers, the school board, community partners, the taxpayers, parents, and above all, the primary customer—the young student. The principal has six constituencies, each of which sees the school differently. Each of them is essential, each defines value differently, and each has to be satisfied at least to the point where they don't fire the principal, go on strike, or rebel.

LISTEN TO YOUR CUSTOMERS

To formulate a successful plan you will need to understand each of your constituencies' concerns, especially what they consider results in the long term. Integrating what customers value into the institution's plan is almost an architectural process, a structural process. It's not too difficult to do once it's understood, but it's hard work. First, think through what knowledge you need to gain. Then listen to customers, accept what they value as objective fact, and make sure the customer's voice is part of your discussions and decisions, not just during the self-assessment process, but continually.

Note

The preceding text is from Peter F. Drucker, *The Drucker Foundation Self-Assessment Tool: Participant Workbook* (San Francisco: Jossey-Bass, 1999), SAT2, pp. 32–34.

Question 3

WHAT DOES THE CUSTOMER VALUE?

Jim Kouzes

Everything exemplary leaders do is about creating value for their customers.

That is exactly the perspective Patricia Maryland took when she came on board as president of Sinai-Grace Hospital, in Detroit, Michigan. When Patricia arrived, she found a hospital in distress. Sinai-Grace was the one hospital remaining after a series of mergers, and all the "slashing and burning" had left the staff feeling angry and distrustful. But even after all the cuts, the hospital was still losing money. Sinai-Grace was an organization not only looking for new leadership but also searching for a new identity.

One of the first things Patricia noticed was that employees mostly related to the way things had been done in the past, and that breaking this deep-seated paradigm would be one of the first tasks Patricia and her team needed to tackle. For example, one obvious challenge was the long waits that patients—the hospital's customers—experienced in the emergency room. "When I first came here, it took people an average of eight hours to be seen and admitted to a hospital bed," Patricia said, "and this was clearly unacceptable."

Another challenge was the way the hospital was perceived by the community. According to Patricia, the perception was that "it was a dirty hospital. There were individuals who lived within a block of us who tended to go to other hospitals. It was clear that the physical environment was a big part of the problem." These kinds of issues demanded immediate action, and because they had existed for so long and were accepted by hospital staff as normal, resolving them required experimenting with some fundamentally new approaches.

To address the unacceptable ER wait times, Patricia challenged the long-standing tradition of how the department was organized. The team accepted the challenge and responded with an innovative new service. "One of the changes we wanted to make was a separate area for chest pain patients so they would be triaged immediately, and our urgent care population could be moved to another area called Express Care." In Express Care, the hospital built examination rooms with walls, improving privacy and confidentiality. These simple changes reduced wait time by more than 75 percent.

Building on this success was a $100,000 foundation grant to upgrade hospital decor. Fresh paint, new carpets, and new furniture can do wonders for the morale of both patients and staff. Patricia got the doctors to donate artwork, and the environment took an immediate turn for the better, beginning to look like a contemporary medical center. "I really felt it was important to create an environment here that was warm, that was embracing, that would allow patients coming in the door to feel some level of trust and comfort," Patricia explained.

Patricia also challenged staff to take a look at the way they related to patients: "If this was your mother you were treating, if this patient was your father, how would you work with them? How would you talk to them? How would you feel if someone was cold, unfriendly, and treated you like you're a piece of machinery rather than a human being?"

These first few changes at Sinai-Grace Hospital started an outstanding turnaround. Customer service scores went up dramatically—from mostly ones and twos on a five-point scale to mostly fours and fives. Today staff morale is high, and there's a new vitality and enthusiasm at Sinai-Grace. And the hospital is now doing quite well financially. Most important, said Patricia, "There's confidence from the community, and they are feeling more comfortable coming back here."

All these improvements were driven by an unyielding commitment to listening to and creating value for the customer. It was Patricia's dedication to first understanding how the hospital's customers experienced Sinai-Grace and then responding to their needs—and enabling staff to do the same—that supported each innovation to restore the health and well-being of the organization, and the morale and pride of the staff. All of this was possible because Patricia and her team had one fundamental purpose in mind: to create extraordinary value for the customer.

So, what does the customer value? Clearly customers value an organization that seeks their feedback and that is capable of solving their problems and meeting their needs. But I would also venture to guess that customers value a leader and a team who have the ability to listen and the courage to challenge the "business-as-usual" environment, all in service of the yearnings of the customer.

❖

What Are Our Results?

Question 4

WHAT ARE OUR RESULTS?

Peter F. Drucker

- ❖ How do we define results?
- ❖ Are we successful?
- ❖ How should we define results?
- ❖ What must we strengthen or abandon?

he results of social sector organizations are always measured *outside* the organization in changed lives and changed conditions—in people's behavior, circumstances, health, hopes, and above all, in their competence and capacity. To further the mission, each nonprofit needs to determine what should be appraised and judged, then concentrate resources for results.

LOOK AT SHORT-TERM ACCOMPLISH-MENTS AND LONG-TERM CHANGE

A small mental health center was founded and directed by a dedicated husband-and-wife team, both psychotherapists. They called it a "healing community," and in the fifteen years they ran the organization, they achieved results others had dismissed as impossible. Their primary customers were people diagnosed with schizophrenia, and most came to the center following failure after failure in treatment, their situation nearly hopeless.

The people at the center said, "There *is* somewhere to turn." Their first measure was whether primary customers and their families were willing to try again. The staff had a number of ways to monitor progress. Did participants regularly attend group sessions and participate fully in daily routines? Did the incidence and length of psychiatric hospitalizations decrease? Could these individuals show new understanding of their disease by saying, "I have had an episode," as opposed to citing demons in the closet? As they progressed, could participants set realistic goals for their own next steps?

The center's mission was *to enable people with serious and persistent mental illness to recover,* and after two or more years of intensive work, many could function in this world—they were no longer "incurable." Some were able to return to a life with their family. Others could hold steady jobs. A few completed graduate school. Whether or not members of that healing community did recover—whether the lives of primary customers changed in this fundamental way—was the organization's single bottom line.

In business, you can debate whether profit is really an adequate measuring stick, but without it, there *is* no business in the long term. In the social sector, no such universal standard for success exists. Each organization must identify its customers, learn what they value, develop meaningful measures, and honestly judge whether, in fact, lives are being changed. This is a new discipline for many nonprofit groups, but it is one that can be learned.

QUALITATIVE AND QUANTITATIVE MEASURES

Progress and achievement can be appraised in *qualitative* and *quantitative* terms. These two types of measures are interwoven—they shed light on one another—and both are necessary to illuminate in what ways and to what extent lives are being changed.

Qualitative measures address the depth and breadth of change within its particular context. They begin with specific observations, build toward patterns, and tell a subtle, individualized story. Qualitative appraisal offers valid, "rich" data. The education director at a major museum tells of the man who sought her out to explain how the museum had opened his teenage mind to new possibilities in a way he knew literally saved his life. She used this result to support her inspiration for a new initiative with troubled youth. The people in a successful research institute cannot quantify the value of their research ahead of time. But they can sit down every three years and ask, "What have we achieved that contributed to changed lives? Where do we focus now for results tomorrow?" Qualitative results can be in the realm of the intangible, such as instilling hope in a patient battling cancer. Qualitative data, although sometimes more subjective and difficult to grasp, are just as real, just as important, and can be gathered just as systematically as the quantitative.

Quantitative measures use definitive standards. They begin with categories and expectations and tell an objective story. Quantitative appraisal offers valid "hard" data. Examples of quantitative measures are as follows: whether overall school performance improves when at-risk youth have intensive arts education; whether the percentage of welfare recipients who complete training and become employed at a livable wage goes up; whether health professionals change their practice based on new research; whether the number of teenagers who smoke goes up or down; whether incidences of child abuse fall when twenty-four-hour crisis care is available. Quantitative measures are essential for assessing whether resources are properly concentrated for results, whether progress is being made, whether lives and communities are changing for the better.

ASSESS WHAT MUST BE STRENGTHENED OR ABANDONED

One of the most important questions for nonprofit leadership is, Do we produce results that are sufficiently outstanding for us to justify putting our resources in this area? Need alone does not justify continuing. Nor does tradition. You must match your mission, your concentration, and your results. Like the New Testament parable of the talents, your job is to invest your resources where the returns are manifold, where you can have success.

To abandon anything is always bitterly resisted. People in any organization are always attached to the obsolete—the things that should have worked but did not, the things that once were productive and no longer are. They are most attached to what in an earlier book (*Managing for Results*, 1964) I called "investments in managerial ego." Yet abandonment comes first. Until that has been accomplished, little else gets done. The acrimonious and emotional debate over what to abandon holds everybody in its grip. Abandoning anything is thus difficult, but only for a fairly short spell. Rebirth can begin once the dead are buried; six months later, everybody wonders, "Why did it take us so long?"

LEADERSHIP IS ACCOUNTABLE

There are times to face the fact that the organization as a whole is not performing—that there are weak results everywhere and little prospect of improving. It may be time to merge or liquidate and put your energies somewhere else. And in some performance areas, whether to strengthen or abandon is not clear. You will need a systematic analysis as part of your plan.

At this point in the self-assessment process, you determine what results for the organization should be and where to concentrate for future success. The mission defines the scope of your responsibility. Leadership is accountable to determine what must be appraised and judged, to protect the organization from squandering resources, and to ensure meaningful results.

Note

The preceding text is from Peter F. Drucker, *The Drucker Foundation Self-Assessment Tool: Participant Workbook* (San Francisco: Jossey-Bass, 1999), SAT2, pp. 40–44.

Question 4

WHAT ARE OUR RESULTS?
Judith Rodin

Peter Drucker wrote nearly fifteen years ago that the "most exciting" development in his half century of work with non-profits was that they had begun to talk not of *needs* but of *results*. This was progress of a very important sort—and Drucker, typically, understated his own role in helping inspire the change.

Drucker's explication of Question 4 clearly and cogently lays out some of the most important subordinate questions in the evaluation of outcomes in the nonprofit sector: What are the prerequisites for our success? How do our partners and beneficiaries experience our work? What are our qualitative as well as quantitative goals? How do we define our results? Do we have the courage to admit failure and let others learn from our mistakes?

I would submit, however, that Drucker's insights in this matter are now sufficiently well understood that he would want us today to go further. The contemporary discussion around evaluation is no longer whether it is worthwhile—it surely is; nor is it around whether quantitative measurements alone are sufficient—surely they are not; nor is it confined to whether failure is admissible—surely we must admit that human efforts, no matter how well intended, must fall short, and that refusal to admit failure and share the knowledge with others only compounds that failure.

Instead, the next question—Question 4A, if you will—asks us how we use our results to play a role in Drucker's Question 5, "What is our plan?"

The Five Most Important Questions proceeds on the implicit premise that our plan is fixed and that the results must flow from it. But the program work of a nonprofit is more iterative than linear. Our plan needs to be designed not only to further our mission but *also to yield measurable results,* so that we can know whether or not the plan is succeeding. Just as Drucker is correct in observing that needs are not enough, that intentions are insufficient, so it is also true that a plan should not be considered complete, or even satisfactory, until it has been constructed in such a way as to produce some measurable outcomes and to build mechanisms, a priori, that allow midcourse corrections based on these results. This work is not like conducting a clinical trial or a randomized controlled experiment, however, where we do not break the code until the end. The goal is to achieve real impact; thus, measuring results is a tool for learning, for self-correcting, in order to reach intended, specified outcomes.

In saying this, we must sail between two shoals, what we might think of as the Scylla and Charybdis of nonprofit planning. On the one hand, we must ensure that our plans are designed in such a way that results can be measured. If necessary to guarantee this, we must even be willing to alter our choices of specific interventions to undertake, avoiding those where, for instance, the defined impact is so unclear and immeasurable as to be beyond our reach. On the other hand, we must also avoid the other shoal—the temptation to undertake only that work most easily quantified, to choose the sort of task that produces outputs, but fails to alter the most important outcomes. In this way, to pursue the metaphor just one phrase further, our voyage is an artistic and not just scientific endeavor.

Drucker begins his discussion of Question 4 by observing, with emphasis in the original, that *"results are the key to our survival"* as institutions. If results are our goal, they must also be our test. What endures from the work of nonprofits is not how hard we try or how clever we may be or even how much we care. Hard work is indispensable to success, of course, in this as in any other field; intelligence is prized in our sector as in all others involving intellectual endeavor; and caring is what has drawn the best people into this line of work. But ultimately what is remembered is how we have been able to improve lives. Peter Drucker understood this profoundly. This is why his question, "What are our results?" resonates today.

❖

What Is Our Plan?

Question 5
WHAT IS OUR PLAN?
Peter F. Drucker

❖ Should the mission be changed?

❖ What are our goals?

The self-assessment process leads to a plan that is a concise summation of the organization's purpose and future direction. The plan encompasses mission, vision, goals, objectives, action steps, a budget, and appraisal. Now comes the point to affirm or change the mission and set long-range goals. Remember, every mission statement has to reflect three things: opportunities, competence, and commitment. It answers the questions, *What is our purpose? Why do we do what we do? What, in the end, do we want to be remembered for?* The mission transcends today but guides today, informs today. It provides the framework for setting goals and mobilizing the resources of the organization for getting the right things done.

The development and formal adoption of mission and goals are fundamental to effective governance of a nonprofit organization and are primary responsibilities of the board. Therefore, these strategic elements of the plan must be approved by the board.

To further the mission, there must be action today and specific aims for tomorrow. Yet planning is not masterminding the future. Any attempt to do so is foolish; the future is unpredictable. In the face of uncertainties, planning defines the particular place you *want* to be and how you intend to get there. Planning does not substitute facts for judgment nor science for leadership. It recognizes the importance of analysis, courage, experience, intuition—even hunch. It is responsibility rather than technique.

GOALS ARE FEW, OVERARCHING, AND APPROVED BY THE BOARD

The most difficult challenge is to agree on the institution's goals—the fundamental long-range direction. Goals are overarching and should be few in number. If you have more than five goals, you have none. You're simply spreading yourself too thin. Goals make it absolutely clear where you will concentrate resources for results—the mark of an organization serious about success. Goals flow from mission, aim the organization where it must go, build on strength, address opportunity, and taken together, outline your desired future.

An option for the plan is a vision statement picturing a future when the organization's goals are achieved and its mission accomplished. The Drucker Foundation's vision is *A society that recognizes the social sector as the leading force in creating healthy communities and improving the quality of life.* I have worked with groups who became intensely motivated by these often-idealistic and poetic statements, whereas others say, "Let's not get carried away." If a vision statement—whether a sentence or a page—helps bring the plan to life, by all means include it.

Here is an example of the vision, mission, and goals for an art museum.

Vision: A city where the world's diverse artistic heritage is prized and whose people seek out art to feed their mind and spirit.

Mission: To bring art and people together.

Goal 1: To conserve the collections and inspire partnerships to seek and acquire exceptional objects.

Goal 2: To enable people to discover, enjoy, and understand art through popular and scholarly exhibitions, community education, and publications.

Goal 3: To significantly expand the museum's audience and strengthen its impact with new and traditional members.

Goal 4: To maintain state-of-the-art facilities, technologies, and operations.

Goal 5: To enhance long-term financial security.

Building around mission and long-term goals is the only way to integrate shorter-term interests. Then management can always ask, "Is an objective leading us toward our basic long-range goal, or is it going to sidetrack us, divert us, make us lose sight of our aims?" St. Augustine said, "One prays for miracles but works for results." Your plan leads you to work for results. It converts intentions into action.

OBJECTIVES ARE MEASURABLE, CONCRETE, AND THE RESPONSIBILITY OF MANAGEMENT

Objectives are the specific and measurable levels of achievement that move the organization toward its goals. The chief executive officer is responsible for development of objectives and action steps and detailed budgets that follow. The board must not act at the level of tactical planning, or it interferes with management's vital ability to be flexible in how goals are achieved. When developing and implementing a plan, the board is accountable for mission, goals, and the allocation of resources to results, and for appraising progress and achievement. Management is accountable for objectives, for action steps, for the supporting budget, as well as for demonstrating effective performance.

FIVE ELEMENTS OF EFFECTIVE PLANS

Abandonment: The first decision is whether to abandon what does not work, what has never worked—the things that have outlived their usefulness and their capacity to contribute. Ask of any program, system, or customer group, "If we were not committed to this today, would we go into it?" If the answer is no, say "How can we get out—fast?"

Concentration: Concentration is building on success, strengthening what *does* work. The best rule is to put your efforts into your successes. You will get maximum results. When you have strong performance is the very time to ask, "Can we set an even higher standard?" Concentration is vital, but it's also very risky. You must choose the right concentrations, or—to use a military term—you leave your flanks totally uncovered.

Innovation: You must also look for tomorrow's success, the true innovations, the diversity that stirs the imagination. What are the opportunities, the new conditions, the emerging issues? Do they fit you? Do you really believe in this? But you have to be careful. Before you go into something new, don't say, "This is how we do it." Say, "Let's find out what this requires. What does the customer value? What is the state of the art? How can we make a difference?" Finding answers to these questions is essential.

Risk taking: Planning always involves decisions on where to take the risks. Some risks you can afford to take—if something goes wrong, it is easily reversible with minor damage. And some decisions may carry great risk, but you cannot afford *not* to take it. You have to balance the short range with the long. If you are too conservative, you miss the opportunity. If you commit too much too fast, there may not be a long run to worry about. There is no formula for these risk-taking decisions. They are entrepreneurial and uncertain, but they must be made.

Analysis: Finally, in planning it is important to recognize when you do *not* know, when you are not yet sure whether to abandon, concentrate, go into something new, or take a particular risk. Then your objective is to conduct an analysis. Before making the final decision, you study a weak but essential performance area, a challenge on the horizon, the opportunity just beginning to take shape.

BUILD UNDERSTANDING AND OWNERSHIP

The plan begins with a mission. It ends with *action steps* and a *budget*. Action steps establish accountability for objectives—who will do what by when—and the budget commits the resources necessary to implement the plan. To build understanding and ownership for the plan, action steps are developed by the people who will carry them out. Everyone with a role should have the opportunity to give input. This looks incredibly slow. But when the plan is completed, the next day everyone understands it. More people in the organization want the new, are committed to it, are ready to act.

The Assessment Team will prepare the final plan for review by the board. Following presentation and discussion, the board chairman will request approval of the mission, goals, and supporting budget. The chairman may request adoption of a vision statement, if one has been developed, as part of the plan. As soon as approval is given, implementation begins.

NEVER REALLY BE SATISFIED

This is the last of the self-assessment questions, and your involvement as a participant soon draws to a close. Appraisal will be ongoing. The organization must monitor progress in achieving goals and meeting objectives, and above all, must measure results in changed lives. You must adjust the plan when conditions change, results are poor, there is a surprise success, or when the customer leads you to a place different from where you imagined.

True self-assessment is never finished. Leadership requires constant resharpening, refocusing, never really being satisfied. I encourage you especially to keep asking the question, *What do we want to be remembered for?* It is a question that induces you to renew yourself—and the organization—because it pushes you to see what you can become.

Note

The preceding text is from Peter F. Drucker, *The Drucker Foundation Self-Assessment Tool: Participant Workbook* (San Francisco: Jossey-Bass, 1999), SAT2, pp. 52–56.

Question 5

WHAT IS OUR PLAN?

V. Kasturi Rangan

Planning is the process of translating the organization's strategic or mission goals to a set of actionable programs, and tracing the path of how those within the organization would meet the goals. In a nutshell, strategy formulation is an exercise in setting goals for the organization and developing a model of how achieving the goals would advance the strategic purpose of the organization. A plan, by contrast, is the action agenda that is aimed at reaching the goal. The biggest mistake organizations make about a "plan" is to cast it in stone as a tactical document, much like a construction drawing with all details filled in for perfect implementation. A business plan is quite different. It is an execution process that feeds back to better strategy making and goal setting. Managers shape it, guide it, adapt it, and learn from it. The following are the central elements to an effective plan.

A Strong Focus on Goals: Organizations of all kinds—whether private or nonprofit—need to have a strong focus on their strategic goals. For a private organization, goals could be about such things as market penetration, new product development, and customer satisfaction. For a nonprofit, the organization's overarching mission must be first translated into something that has operational traction, before strategic goals can be set. Whereas the overarching mission might be broad and inspirational, the operating mission must be narrow enough to allow the organization to measure its progress against goals.

Steadfast in Direction, Flexible in Execution: A museum that aims to boost attendance, for example, might plan a series of special exhibitions to attract new or repeat visitors. But an effective plan must go further. It must detail the nature of the planned special exhibitions, their timing, and the promotional programs to draw in the audience. The pitch may differ depending on whether it is new or repeat audiences that the museum wishes to attract. But here lies an important caveat. "Planning is not masterminding the future. Any attempt to do so is foolish; the future is unpredictable," wrote Peter Drucker in the last edition of this self-assessment tool. That's why it is crucially important to keep an open mind regarding the several potential alternative ways of getting to the goal, even while staying steadfast regarding the strategic direction.

For example, in the midst of its promotion, if the program team discovers that its exhibits seem to be attracting much higher numbers of new-to-the-museum visitors than expected, then it must show enough flexibility in its plans to allocate a higher proportion of its resources to convert these new visitors to members. Fresh initiatives may have to be constructed midstream to solidify this opportunistic gain in new visitors. At the same time, it is very important to understand the underlying reasons for this unexpected gain. Only by learning why and absorbing the lessons will the team be able to transfer the gains to future special exhibition programs. By the same token, by learning about plans that have gone awry, an organization will avoid expensive future mistakes. Flexibility and a learning attitude have to be two important characteristics of an effective plan.

Ownership and Accountability Placed with Individuals: The persons responsible for executing a program should be primarily involved in constructing the plan of action. The team could receive inputs from any number of sources, but ultimately the authority for its execution, and ownership for its success or failure should rest with named individuals. That's why it is not useful to impose a detailed planning blueprint from a central station. Once the implementation team has internalized the strategic goals and direction (perhaps some of its members playing a part in formulating them in the first place), they should be given leeway to develop the action plan. This is the only way motivated managers will experience the freedom to scale successful programs, and introspective managers will exercise judgment in reorienting or scaling down not-so-successful programs.

Monitoring That Leads to Better Strategy: The main purpose of monitoring the execution is to understand the logic of each program and its connections to other programs in delivering the strategic goals of an organization. Even when the overall goals of an organization are being met, it is not at all unusual for some programs to be wildly successful and others to fall short. That's why it is not sufficient to monitor the overall attainment of the strategic goals by themselves, but to dig in to find out which programs really contributed to its success and which ones did not, and why. Only through reflection can there be improvements to the next round of strategy development. Such an exercise should be conducted continuously over the planning cycle and always involve the program managers as well as those at a level higher than the individual program teams. The team that was the architect of the strategic direction and goals should be responsible for closing this final feedback loop. This will then serve as a platform for the next planning cycle.

TRANSFORMATIONAL LEADERSHIP

Frances Hesselbein

In a world where the rules are constantly changing, millions of people in every sector of the economy are wrestling with the new demands of leadership. I hear managers everywhere discussing the same fundamental challenge: the journey to transformation, moving from where we are to where we want to be in the tenuous future that lies before us. Around the world—in universities, the community of faith, corporations, government, and the burgeoning social sector—leaders are working to shape the transformation of their institutions.

A few years ago, I ventured to China with a team of four thought leaders to deliver a series of seminars at the invitation of the Bright China Management Institute. As we talked with our Chinese colleagues, we used the same language to describe the power of mission that we use when we work with the Salvation Army, the United States Army, Chevron, or the American Institute of Architects: vision, mission, goals. The actual words are different in every language, but the power of those words is universal. And with a common language, people in every sector, in every culture, can have dialogues of great meaning that help transform organizations.

In sharing experiences across the public, private, and social sectors, I have found that organizations usually pass eight milestones to reach their destination: a relevant, viable, effective organization. These milestones are as relevant to a small community group or the Girl Scouts as they are to a large business or government agency.

1. Scan the environment. Through reading, surveys, interviews, and so on, we identify the major trends likely to affect the organization. The essence of strategy is to define the implications of those trends. Sometimes we can catch a straw in the wind and have a responsive program or project ready as the trend emerges—not after. This assessment of emerging trends and implications, supplemented by internal data, provides essential background for planning change—and offers a better basis for action than our own preconceptions. Flying on assumptions can be fatal.

2. Revisit the mission. At the Leader to Leader Institute, we review our mission every three years, and refine it if necessary. The foundation is now more than fifteen years old, and we've revisited and refined our mission twice—not because we couldn't get it right the first time, with Peter F.

Drucker in the room, but because the environment and the needs of our customers had changed.

The mission statement should simply explain why we do what we do, our reason for being—our purpose. Knowing that management is a tool, not an end, we manage not for the sake of managing in its own right, but for the mission. And one's mission does not define how one operates, but simply why. It must be clear, powerful, compelling, and to the point. The mission of the International Red Cross—"To serve the most vulnerable"—is a perfect example of clarity and power.

When we revisit the mission, we ask ourselves the first three of the five most important questions that Peter Drucker helped organizations answer for more than fifty years:

- What is our mission?
- Who is our customer?
- What does the customer value?

When we answer these, we are well on our way to managing for the mission.

3. Ban the hierarchy. Transformation requires moving people out of their organizational boxes into flexible, fluid management systems. We cannot continue to put people into little squares on a structure chart. Psychologically it boxes them in. I prefer circles—concentric circles of functions and positions in a staffing design that looks almost organic. Job rotation becomes an enriching reality. People move in circular ways—learning new skills, expanding positions. We need to ban a hierarchy not suited to today's knowledge workers, "who carry their toolkits in their heads."

4. Challenge the gospel. There should be no sacred cows as we challenge every policy, practice, procedure, and assumption. In transforming themselves, organizations must practice "planned abandonment"—discarding programs, policies, and practices that work today but have little relevance to the future and to the organization we are building to meet that future.

5. Employ the power of language. Leaders must beam a few clear, consistent messages over and over. They must lead by voice, communicating with all their customers, all their constituents, a few powerful messages that connect and illuminate. When, for example, Max De Pree led his company, Herman Miller, to world leadership, he spoke about workers needing "a covenant, not a contract." Such powerful aspirations—and the language to go with them—are essential to guide an organization into transformation.

6. Disperse leadership across the organization. Every organization must have not one but many leaders. Some speak of "empowerment"; others of "sharing the tasks of leadership." I think of it as dispersing leadership—with leaders developed and performing across every level of the organization. Leadership is a responsibility shared by all members of the organization.

7. *Lead from the front, don't push from the rear.* The leader of the future does not sit on the fence, waiting to see which way the wind is blowing. The leader articulates clear positions on issues affecting the organization and is the embodiment of the enterprise, of its values and principles. Leaders model desired behaviors, never break a promise, and know that leadership is a matter of how to be, not how to do it.

8. *Assess performance.* Self-assessment is essential to progress. From the beginning of the change process, we are clear about mission, goals, and objectives. Well-defined action steps and a plan for measuring results are essential to planning any organizational change. We then can embark on the journey with goals and measures in place. At the end of the process, the most exuberant phase of the journey, we evaluate our performance and celebrate the transformation. We do this by asking the next two of Peter Drucker's five critical questions discussed earlier:

- What are our results?
- What is our plan?

❖

Across the globe, for leaders aware of the tenuous times ahead, the journey to transformation is a journey into the future. These leaders are taking today's organization and transforming it into tomorrow's productive, high-performance enterprise. Although the milestones on the journey are known, the destinations are uncharted, and for each organization the destination will be determined not only by the curve of the road ahead but also by the quality of the mission and the leadership it inspires.

THE SELF-ASSESSMENT PROCESS

Peter F. Drucker

The *Self-Assessment Tool* was intentionally developed as a flexible resource. How you use this book will depend on your setting and the particular purpose for which self-assessment is being undertaken. The Workbook has not arrived on your doorstep on its own. It is in your hands because you have an interest in it or an Assessment Team, an instructor, a manager, or leader has thought through a self-assessment process design, identified a role for you, and asked you to participate. It is the responsibility of that team or individual to explain the purpose for self-assessment and to orient you to specific time and task expectations.

The self-assessment process calls for broad participation to ensure understanding, ownership, and readiness to act. Certain adaptations of the self-assessment process are discrete and may be completed within a matter of weeks.

Comprehensive self-assessment for an organization takes place in three phases over a number of months. A detailed Process Guide shows those leading self-assessment how to properly organize and direct it.

This Workbook has a twofold purpose: *(1) to guide your individual thinking and (2) to prepare you and others for productive discussion and decision making.* To make the most of what is offered here, you will do three things:

1. Thoroughly review the information that is provided on your organization, its customers, trends in its operating environment, and other self-assessment materials or reports.
2. Sit down with this Workbook and, in one or more sessions, take the necessary time to read it through and give a thoughtful response to the important questions it asks.
3. Actively participate in a retreat, group discussions, a one-to-one depth interview, or in other self-assessment meetings.

My final word on how to use this book: Please don't rush through it at the last minute. The five questions appear simple, but they are not. Give them time to sink in; wrestle over them. Properly carried through, self-assessment develops skill, competence, and commitment. Active and attentive participation is an opportunity to enhance your vision and *to shape the future.*

Note

The preceding text is from Peter F. Drucker, *The Drucker Foundation Self-Assessment Tool: Participant Workbook* (San Francisco: Jossey-Bass, 1999), SAT2, pp. 7–8.

SUGGESTED
QUESTIONS TO
EXPLORE

The most important aspect of the *Self-Assessment Tool* is the questions it poses. Answers are important; you need answers because you need action. But the most important thing is to ask these questions.

—Peter F. Drucker[1]

QUESTION 1: WHAT IS OUR MISSION?

As you work through the overarching question "What is our mission?" consider the following additional questions—they may help you find the answers you seek:

What are we trying to achieve?[2]

- What is your organization's current understanding of the organization's mission?[3]

- What is your organization's reason for being?[4]
- Why do you do what you do?[5]
- For what, in the end, do you want to be remembered?[6]

What are the significant external or internal challenges, opportunities, and issues?

- What significant challenges is the organization facing—changing demographics, legislation or regulations, emerging technologies, competition?
- What significant opportunities are presenting themselves—partnerships and collaborations, leading-edge practices or approaches, social or cultural trends?
- What are the emerging critical issues for the organization—need for multilingual employees, community-based issues, market share, rising cost of health care, changing distribution channels?

Does our mission need to be revisited?[7]

- Does the mission statement need to be redefined? If not, why not? If yes, why is that?[8]
- In what ways, if any, would you rewrite or refocus the mission statement for your organization?[9]
- What would be the major benefits of a new mission? Why do you say that?[10]
- What problems, if any, would you be likely to encounter with the new mission? Among whom? Why is that? What steps, if any, may need to be taken to effect this change?[11]

QUESTION 2: WHO IS OUR CUSTOMER?

As you work through the overarching question "Who is our customer?" consider the following additional questions—they may help you find the answers you seek:

Who are our customers?

- Create a list of those who use the organization's products or services. For nonprofits, from that list identify who is the primary customer—the people whose lives are changed through the organization's work. For businesses, from the list identify who the primary customer is currently and determine if that customer can and will sustain the organization based on demographic potential and so on. For public institutions, often the primary customer is determined through legislation or by the government authority establishing the organization.
- Create a list of supporting customers—the volunteers, members, partners, funders, referral sources, employees, and others—both inside and outside the organization who must be satisfied.
- What value do we provide each of these customers?[12]
- Do our strengths, our competencies, and resources match the needs of these customers? If yes, in what way? If not, why not?[13]

Have our customers changed?[14]

- In what ways, if any, have your customers changed? Think in terms of . . .[15]

89

- Demographics? (age, sex, race, ethnicity)[16]
- Primary needs? (training, shelter, day care, and so on)[17]
- Number? (greater, fewer)[18]
- Physical and psychological well-being? (such as drug dependence, family dysfunction)[19]
- Other ways? (for example, location, workplace)[20]
- What are the implications of these changes for your organization?[21]

Should we add or delete some customers?[22]

- What *other groups* of customers, if any, *should the organization be serving*? Why is that?[23]
- What special competencies does the organization have to benefit them?[24]
- What *groups of current customers*, if any, *should the organization no longer serve*?[25]
- Why is that? (Their needs have changed? Your resources are too limited? Other organizations are more effective? Their needs do not fit your organization's mission? Its competencies?)[26]

QUESTION 3: WHAT DOES THE CUSTOMER VALUE?

As you work through the overarching question "What does the customer value?" consider the following additional questions—they may help you find the answers you seek:

What do our customers value?[27]

- Think about value in terms of what your organization does that fills a specific need, provides satisfaction, or offers a benefit to your primary customers that they do not receive from another source. For each group of primary customers . . . briefly describe what each values about your organization.[28]
- Think about value in terms of what your organization does that fills a specific need, provides satisfaction, or offers a benefit to your secondary customers that they do not receive from another source. For each group of supporting customers . . . briefly describe what each values about your organization.[29]
- What are our customers' long-term aspirations, and what is our capacity and competency to deliver on those aspirations?
- How well does your organization provide what each of your customers considers value?[30]
- How can the knowledge you have about what your customers consider value be used to make decisions in areas like those listed?[31]
  - Products or services
  - Recruitment
  - Training
  - Innovation
  - Fund development
  - Marketing
  - Other

- What resources—internal and external—can you use to determine your customers' level of satisfaction? For example, do you need to conduct a survey of current customers as well as those who no longer use your service?[32]
- What do our *supporting* customers consider value?[33]
- If they are donors, do they value recognition or a sense that their contribution is helping solve a community problem?
- If they are volunteers, do they give of their time because they seek to learn new skills, make new friends, feel that they are helping to change lives?
- If they are related to the primary customer, do we know what their expectations are, as related to their family member?
- If they are distributors or members of the supply chain for our product or service, what are their needs and constraints related to their mission, profitability, and goals?

QUESTION 4: WHAT ARE OUR RESULTS?

As you work through the overarching question "What are our results?" consider the following additional questions—they may help you find the answers you seek:

How do we define results for our organization?[34]

- Having thought through the first three Drucker questions on Mission, Customers, and Value . . .

would you define "results" any differently? Why or why not?[35]

- How would you define results in the future?

To what extent have we achieved these results?[36]

- Considering your responses [to the questions in the previous section], to what extent has your organization achieved these results?[37]
- What are the major activities or programs that have helped (or hindered) the achievement of these results?[38]
- How will you measure results in the future, both qualitatively and quantitatively?

How well are we using our resources?[39]

- How well is your organization using its human resources—its volunteers, board, staff, and so on? How do you know that? What *should* the organization be doing?[40]
- How well is your organization using its financial resources—such as its money, buildings, investments, gifts? How do you know that? What *should* the organization be doing?[41]
- How effectively are we attending to the value and positioning of our brand and our brand promise?
- What have been the results of your organization's efforts to attract and keep donors? Why is that?[42]
- How does the organization define and share its results with the donors? In what ways, if any, should it change its procedures? Why or why not?[43]

- Are other, similar organizations doing a better job of using their human and financial resources? Of attracting and satisfying donors? Of using their board? If yes, why is that? What can you learn from them?[44]

QUESTION 5: WHAT IS OUR PLAN?

As you work through the overarching question "What is our plan?" consider the following additional questions—they may help you find the answers you seek:

What have we learned, and what do we recommend?[45]

- List the most important lessons and summarize the actions they suggest.[46]
- Think about information that will help not only in the area for which you have responsibility but also in planning for the future direction and activities of the organization.[47]

Where should we focus our efforts?[48]

- List those areas where you believe *your group or area of responsibility* should be focused. Briefly state your reasons and how each one fits the mission.[49]
- Given what you have learned, list those areas where you believe *your organization* should be focused. Next, briefly state your reasons and how each one fits the mission.[50]

What, if anything, should we do differently?[51]

- Are there programs, activities, or customer needs that the organization should add?[52]
- Abandon?[53]
- Refer to other organizations, that is, "outsource" if it is unable to handle them effectively or efficiently in-house?[54]
- Why is that?[55]

What is our plan to achieve results for the organization?[56]

- What are the goals that will enable us to achieve the desired results?
- For nonprofits, what are the goals (fundamental aims) that will change lives and help us further the mission?
- What are the measurable objectives that will enable us to achieve our goals?
- What are the measurable action steps that will enable us to achieve our objectives?
- What are the budget implications of the resources required to achieve these goals, objectives, and action steps?
- What are the target dates for completion?
- Who will be responsible and accountable for achieving each goal, objective, and action step?
- What staffing will be needed to support this plan?
- How do we evaluate and measure the desired results?

What is my plan to achieve results for my group or responsibility area?[57]

- Make a list of action items you have the authority to enact as well as those recommendations that need to be approved by appropriate board and staff teams.[58]
- Then establish a target date for approval and implementation.[59]
- Identify staff support needed.[60]

Notes

Where indicated with endnotes, the preceding text is from Peter F. Drucker, *The Five Most Important Questions You Will Ever Ask About Your Nonprofit Organization* (San Francisco: Jossey-Bass, 1993), SAT1. The endnotes specify the source page numbers. See facing page.

The text *not* attributed to Peter F. Drucker in the form of an endnote was contributed by trainers Maria Carpenter Ort and Tamara Woodbury—who have worked extensively with Drucker's *The Five Most Important Questions You Will Ever Ask About Your Nonprofit Organization*—along with project editor Peter Economy to address common situations not covered in Drucker's original text.

DEFINITIONS
OF TERMS

Action steps: Detailed plans and activities directed toward meeting an organization's objectives.

Appraisal: Process for monitoring progress in meeting objectives and achieving results; point at which the plans for meeting objectives may be modified, based on experience or changed conditions.

Budget: The commitment of resources necessary to implement plans—the financial expression of a particular plan of work.

Customers: Those who must be satisfied in order for the organization to achieve results. The *primary customer* is the person whose life is changed through the organization's work. *Supporting customers* are volunteers, members, partners, funders, referral sources, employees, and others who must be satisfied.

Customer value: That which satisfies customers' *needs* (physical and psychological well-being), *wants* (where, when, and how service is provided), and *aspirations* (desired long-term results).

Depth interviews: One-on-one interviews used to highlight the insights of a select group of individuals inside the organization. Interview findings provide a touchstone for group discussions and decision making.

Goals: A set of three to five aims that set the organization's fundamental, long-range direction.

Mission: Why you do what you do; the organization's reason for being, its purpose. Says what, in the end, you want to be remembered for.

Objectives: Specific and measurable levels of achievement.

Plan: Your proposed approach to achieving the organization's goals, objectives, and action steps. To be effective, plans must contain firm target dates for completion; specific individuals who will be responsible and accountable for achievement and completion of goals, objectives, and action steps; and necessary human (people) and financial (money) resources.*

Results: The organization's bottom line. Defined in *changed lives*—people's behavior, circumstances, health, hopes, competence, or capacity. Results are always *outside* the organization.

Vision: A picture of the organization's desired future.

Note

Except for (*), the preceding text is from Peter F. Drucker, *The Drucker Foundation Self-Assessment Tool: Participant Workbook* (San Francisco: Jossey-Bass, 1999), SAT2, pp. 9–10.

ABOUT THE CONTRIBUTORS

Jim Collins is one of the greatest thought leaders of his generation. He is a student and teacher of enduring great companies—how they grow, how they attain superior performance, and how good companies can become great companies. He is the author of such business classics as *Good to Great* and *Built to Last* and the monograph *Good to Great and the Social Sectors*. Visit his Web site at www.jimcollins.com.

❖

Philip Kotler is the S. C. Johnson & Son Distinguished Professor of International Marketing at the Northwestern University Kellogg Graduate School of Management in Chicago and the coauthor with Nancy Lee of the book *Corporate Social Responsibility: Doing the Most Good for Your Company and Cause*. Visit the Kotler Marketing Group Web site at www.kotlermarketing.com.

❖

Jim Kouzes is the coauthor with Barry Posner of the award-winning and best-selling book *The Leadership Challenge,* with over one million copies sold. He is also an executive fellow at the Center for Innovation and Entrepreneurship, Leavey School of Business, Santa Clara University. Visit the Kouzes-Posner Web site at www.kouzesposner.com.

❖

Judith Rodin has served as president of the Rockefeller Foundation since March 2005. A groundbreaking research psychologist, Dr. Rodin was previously the president of the University of Pennsylvania, the first woman to lead an Ivy League institution, and earlier the provost of Yale University. Visit the Rockefeller Foundation Web site at www.rockfound.org.

❖

V. Kasturi Rangan is the Malcolm P. McNair Professor of Marketing at the Harvard Business School and coauthor with Marie Bell of *Transforming Your Go-to-Market Strategy: The Three Disciplines of Channel Management.* Until recently the chairman of the Marketing Department (1998–2002), he is now the cochairman of the school's Social Enterprise Initiative. Visit the Harvard Business School Web site at www.hbs.edu.

❖

Frances Hesselbein is the founding president and chairman of the Leader to Leader Institute, formerly the Peter F. Drucker Foundation for Nonprofit Management. She served as CEO of the Girl Scouts of the USA and was awarded the Presidential Medal of Freedom. She is the author of *Hesselbein on Leadership;* coeditor of twenty other books, including *Be, Know, Do;* and the editor in chief of the award-winning journal *Leader to Leader.*

ABOUT THE LEADER TO LEADER INSTITUTE

Established in 1990 as the Peter F. Drucker Foundation for Nonprofit Management, the Leader to Leader Institute furthers its mission—to strengthen the leadership of the social sector—by providing social sector leaders with essential leadership wisdom, inspiration, and resources to lead for innovation and to build vibrant social sector organizations. It is this essential social sector, in collaboration with its partners in the private and public sectors, that changes lives and builds a society of healthy children, strong families, good schools, decent housing, safe neighborhoods, and work that dignifies, all embraced by the diverse, inclusive, cohesive community that cares about all its people.

The Leader to Leader Institute provides innovative and relevant resources, products, and experiences that enable leaders of the future to address emerging opportunities and challenges. With the goal of leading social sector organizations toward excellence in performance, the Institute has brought together more than four hundred great thought leaders to publish twenty-three books available in twenty-eight languages, and the quarterly journal, *Leader to Leader*. This Apex Award–winning journal is the essential leadership resource for leaders in business, government, and the social sectors—leaders of the future.

The Leader to Leader Institute engages social sector leaders in partnerships across the sectors that provide new and significant opportunities for learning and growth. It coordinates unique, high-level summits for leaders from all three sectors and collaborates on workshops and conferences for social sector leaders on leadership, self-assessment, and cross-sector partnerships.

Building on its legacy of innovation, the Leader to Leader Institute explores new approaches to strengthen the leadership of the social sector. With sources of talent and inspiration that range from the local community development corporation to the U.S. Army to the corporate boardroom, the Institute helps social sector organizations identify new leaders and new ways of managing that embrace change and abandon the practices of yesterday that no longer achieve results today.

ACKNOWLEDGMENTS

We at the Leader to Leader Institute wish to express our deepest appreciation to all those who helped bring this work to fruition: Peter Drucker, Jim Collins, Philip Kotler, Jim Kouzes, Judith Rodin, V. Kasturi Rangan, Frances Hesselbein, Peter Economy, Jeong Bae, Jeannie Radbill, Maria Carpenter Ort, Tamara Woodbury, Peggy Outon, Bruce and Anne Turley, Dr. Denice Rothman Hinden, and the attendees of the 2006 Self-Assessment Tool revision planning retreat and of the 2007 Self-Assessment Tool review, and to Constance Rossum for her contributions to the writing of the first edition of *The Five Most Important Questions* tool in 1993.

And we are deeply grateful to three very close and trusted friends and colleagues of the late Peter Drucker who contributed funding to publish and promote this edition of the Self-Assessment Tool: Bob Buford, Bill Pollard, and David Jones. From the bottom of our hearts we thank you. We could not have accomplished this important undertaking without your support and friendship, and your generosity will have an impact on lives around the world for years to come.

ADDITIONAL RESOURCES

The Leader to Leader Institute
- www.leadertoleader.org
- Frances Hesselbein & Alan Shrader, *Leader to Leader 2: Enduring Insights on Leadership from the Leader to Leader Institute's Award-Winning Journal*. San Francisco: Jossey-Bass, 2007
- Frances Hesselbein & Marshall Goldsmith, *The Leader of the Future 2: Visions, Strategies, and Practices for the New Era*. San Francisco: Jossey-Bass, 2006

The Leader to Leader Self-Assessment Tool
- Visit the tool at www.fivequestionsbook.com
- James G. Dalton, Jennifer Jarratt, & John Mahaffie, *From Scan to Plan: Integrating Trends into the Strategy Making Process*. Washington, D.C.: ASAE and the Center for Association Leadership, 2003
- www.asaecenter.org/files/FileDownloads/FromScanto Plan.pdf

Peter F. Drucker

- www.druckerarchives.net
- Peter F. Drucker & Joseph A. Maciarello, *The Effective Executive in Action: A Journal for Getting the Right Things Done.* New York: HarperBusiness, 2005
- Peter F. Drucker, *The Essential Drucker: The Best of Sixty Years of Peter Drucker's Essential Writings on Management.* New York: HarperBusiness, 2003
- Peter F. Drucker, *Managing in a Time of Great Change.* New York: Truman Tally Books, 1995
- Peter F. Drucker, *Management: Tasks, Responsibilities, Practices.* New York: HarperBusiness, 1993
- Peter F. Drucker, *Managing the Non-Profit Organization: Practices and Principles.* New York: HarperCollins, 1992

Jim Collins

- www.jimcollins.com
- Jim Collins, *Good to Great and the Social Sectors.* New York: HarperCollins, 2005
- Jim Collins, *Good to Great: Why Some Companies Make the Leap . . . and Others Don't.* New York: HarperBusiness, 2001
- Jim Collins & Jerry Porras, *Built to Last: Successful Habits of Visionary Companies.* New York: HarperBusiness, 1994

Philip Kotler

- www.kotlermarketing.com
- Philip Kotler & Kevin Lane Keller, *Marketing Management, 12th Edition.* Upper Saddle River, N.J.: Prentice Hall, 2005
- Philip Kotler, *According to Kotler: The World's Foremost Authority on Marketing Answers Your Questions.* New York: AMACOM, 2005
- Philip Kotler & Nancy Lee, *Corporate Social Responsibility: Doing the Most Good for Your Company and Cause.* Hoboken, N.J.: Wiley, 2004
- Philip Kotler, *Kotler on Marketing: How to Create, Win, and Dominate Markets.* New York: Free Press, 2001

Jim Kouzes

- www.kouzesposner.com
- James M. Kouzes & Barry Z. Posner, *The Leadership Challenge, 4th Edition.* San Francisco: Jossey-Bass, 2007
- James M. Kouzes & Barry Z. Posner, *A Leader's Legacy.* San Francisco: Jossey-Bass, 2006
- James M. Kouzes & Barry Z. Posner, *Encouraging the Heart: A Leader's Guide to Rewarding and Recognizing Others.* San Francisco: Jossey-Bass, 2003

Judith Rodin

- www.rockfound.org
- Judith Rodin, *The University and Urban Revival: Out of the Ivory Tower and into the Streets*. Philadelphia: University of Pennsylvania Press, 2007
- Judith Rodin & Stephen P. Steinberg, editors, *Public Discourse in America: Conversation and Community in the Twenty-First Century*. Philadelphia: University of Pennsylvania Press, 2003

V. Kasturi Rangan

- http://hbswk.hbs.edu/faculty/vrangan.html
- V. Kasturi Rangan & Marie Bell, *Transforming Your Go-to-Market Strategy: The Three Disciplines of Channel Management*. Boston: Harvard Business School Press, 2006
- Rajiv Lal, John Quelch, & V. Kasturi Rangan, *Marketing Management: Text and Cases*. New York: McGraw-Hill, 2004

INDEX